HEALTH HELPERS

I NEED AN EYE DOCTOR

By Rachel Rose

Consultant: Beth Gambro
Reading Specialist, Yorkville, Illinois

Minneapolis, Minnesota

Teaching Tips

Before Reading

- Look at the cover of the book. Discuss the picture and the title.
- Ask readers to brainstorm a list of what they already know about eye doctors. What can they expect to see in the book?
- Go on a picture walk, looking through the pictures to discuss vocabulary and make predictions about the text.

During Reading

- Read for purpose. Encourage readers to think about the kinds of things that might make us need an eye doctor.
- Ask readers to look for the details of the book. How can an eye doctor help?
- If readers encounter an unknown word, ask them to look at the sounds in the word. Then, ask them to look at the rest of the page. Are there any clues to help them understand?

After Reading

- Encourage readers to pick a buddy and reread the book together.
- Ask readers to name two things they might find at an eye doctor's office. Find the pages that tell about these things.
- Ask readers to write or draw something they learned about eye doctors as health helpers.

Credits

Cover and title page, © Gelpi/Adobe Stock and © runna10/iStock; 3, © DenKuvaiev/iStock; 5, © SolStock/iStock and © 1shot Production/iStock; 6–7, © SDI Productions/iStock; 8–9, © FluxFactory/iStock; 11, © Yistocking/Adobe Stock; 13, © eakgrungenerd/Adobe Stock; 15, © Pavel/Adobe Stock; 17, © chingyunsong/iStock; 18–19, © Hispanolistic/iStock; 21, © AntonioDiaz/Adobe Stock; 22TL, © serikbaib/iStock; 22TM, © Pixel-Shot/Adobe Stock; 22TR, © terex/iStock; 22BL, © Liza888/Shutterstock; 22BR, © Garrett Aitken/iStock; 23TL, © saras66/iStock; 23TM, © Pixel-Shot/Adobe Stock; 23TR, © katleho Seisa/iStock; 23BL, © ijeab/iStock; 23BR, © Krakenimages.com/Shutterstock.

See BearportPublishing.com for our statement on Generative AI Usage.

Library of Congress Cataloging-in-Publication Data

Names: Rose, Rachel, 1968- author.
Title: I need an eye doctor / by Rachel Rose.
Description: Minneapolis, Minnesota : Bearport Publishing Company, [2025] |
  Series: Health helpers | Includes bibliographical references and index.
Identifiers: LCCN 2024021906 (print) | LCCN 2024021907 (ebook) | ISBN
  9798892326346 (library binding) | ISBN 9798892327145 (paperback) | ISBN
  9798892326742 (ebook)
Subjects: LCSH: Ophthalmologists--Juvenile literature. |
  Optometrists--Juvenile literature. | Ophthalmology--Juvenile literature.
  | Optometry--Juvenile literature.
Classification: LCC RE52 .R67 2025 (print) | LCC RE52 (ebook) | DDC
  617.7--dc23/eng/20240621
LC record available at https://lccn.loc.gov/2024021906
LC ebook record available at https://lccn.loc.gov/2024021907

Copyright © 2025 Bearport Publishing Company. All rights reserved. No part of this publication may be reproduced in whole or in part, stored in any retrieval system, or transmitted in any form or by any means, electronic, mechanical, photocopying, recording, or otherwise, without written permission from the publisher.

For more information, write to Bearport Publishing, 5357 Penn Avenue South, Minneapolis, MN 55419.

Contents

An Eye Doctor Helps 4

Eye Doctor Tools 22

Glossary 23

Index 24

Read More 24

Learn More Online.......................... 24

About the Author 24

An Eye Doctor Helps

The board looks **blurry**.

Uh-oh!

I cannot see what it says.

Who can help me?

I need an eye doctor!

The eye doctor is busy.

I have to wait.

Then, it is my turn.

The doctor takes me back to a room.

I am a little **nervous**.

But the doctors says nothing will hurt.

Phew!

I feel safe.

I sit in a big chair.

The eye doctor has a small light.

It is bright.

The light helps them see into my eyes.

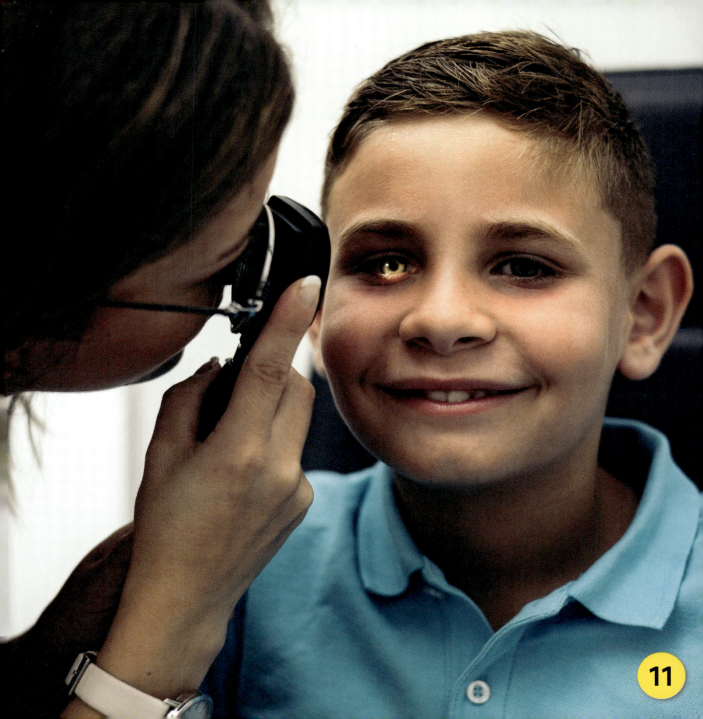

The doctor takes out a special tool.

It looks like a big spoon.

They cover one of my eyes with it.

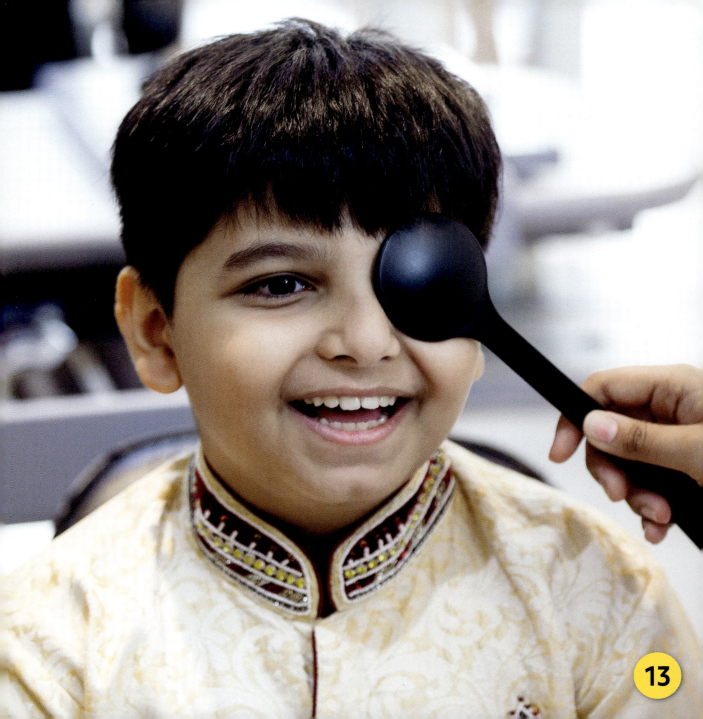

The eye doctor shows me a **chart**.

I see a star!

But other parts are blurry.

I need glasses.

I look into a big **machine**.

Click!

How does the chart look now?

That is much better!

I can see everything.

It is time to try on glasses.

There are lots of **frames** to pick from.

Some are round.

Others look like squares.

I like these glasses.

They are fun!

I can see better now, too.

Thanks, eye doctor!

Eye Doctor Tools

An eye doctor uses many tools.

22

Glossary

blurry fuzzy or not clear

chart a sheet or board that shows pictures

frames things that hold glasses in place

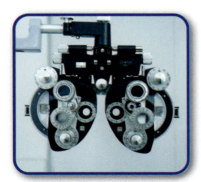

machine a thing with moving parts

nervous feeling afraid or scared

Index

chart 14, 16
frames 18
glasses 14, 18, 20
light 10
machine 16–17
spoon 12

Read More

Brinker, Spencer. *Doctors (What Makes a Community?)*. Minneapolis: Bearport Publishing, 2021.

Leed, Percy. *The Sense of Sight: A First Look (Read about Senses)*. Minneapolis: Lerner Publications, 2023.

Learn More Online

1. Go to **FactSurfer.com** or scan the QR code below.
2. Enter "**Need Eye Doctor**" into the search box.
3. Click on the cover of this book to see a list of websites.

About the Author

Rachel Rose loves to read, so she takes care of her eyes!